BUSINESS CYCLES IN THE POSTWAR WORLD

Some Reflections on Recent Research

Philip A. Klein

American Enterprise Institute for Public Policy Research
Washington, D. C.

Philip A. Klein is professor of economics at The Pennsylvania State University, a member of the research staff of the National Bureau of Economic Research, and an adjunct scholar of the American Enterprise Institute.

Domestic Affairs Study 42, February 1976

ISBN 0-8447-3201-X

Library of Congress Catalog Card No. 76-316

Printed in the United States of America

For Kathleen and Alan

The uncertainty attending forecasts arises chiefly from the imperfections of our knowledge concerning business conditions in the immediate past and in the present. For, since business cycles result from processes of cumulative change, the main factors in shaping tomorrow are the factors that were at work yesterday and are at work today.

Wesley Clair Mitchell, *Business Cycles*, 1913

CONTENTS

INTRODUCTION AND SUMMARY   1

I   CLASSICAL CYCLES   2
   The National Bureau's Point of Departure   4
   A Current Perspective   6

II   GROWTH CYCLES: NEW WINE OR NEW BOTTLES?   12
   The Rediscovery of the Growth Cycle   12
   Is the Growth Cycle Obsolete?   18
   Developing Chronologies   21

III   THE INTERNATIONAL TRANSMISSION OF INSTABILITY   27
   Of Sneezes and Colds   31
   Is There an International Business Cycle?   41

CONCLUSIONS   43

APPENDIX   45

LIST OF TABLES

1. Classical-Cycle Turning Points in Four Countries, 1792–1961   8
2. The 1973–1975 Contraction Compared with Three Preceding Contractions   10
3. Comparison of Growth-Cycle and Classical-Cycle Turning Points, United States, 1948–1970   15
4. Comparison of Turning Points in Alternative Growth-Cycle Chronologies, United States, 1948–1973   20

5. Timing Comparison of Six Roughly Coincident Indicators at Classical-Cycle and Growth-Cycle Turning Points, United States, 1948–1970 22

6. Postwar Growth-Cycle Chronologies for Five Countries with Leads (−) and Lags (+) in Comparison with the United States, 1948–1973 24

7. Comparison of Matched Turns in Cycles, United Kingdom and United States, (W.) Germany and United States, with U.S. Turns as Reference Chronology, Selected Periods, 1854–1972 30

8. Amounts of Change in U.S.-U.K. Export Trade During Growth Cycles, 1951–1973 33

9. Amounts of Change in U.S.-Canadian Export Trade During Cycles, 1950–1973 35

10. Rates of Change in U.S.-Japanese Export Trade During Cycles, 1952–1973 36

11. Rates of Change in U.S.-W. German Export Trade During Cycles, 1951–73 38

12. Summary: Rates of Change in Trade Between United States and Four Developed Countries During Growth Cycles 39

13. Consensus Peaks and Troughs in Growth Rates as Measured by Four Measures of Economic Activity, Eight Countries Outside the United States and the United States, 1953–1973   42

A-1. Detailed Information on Timing Comparisons, United States and United Kingdom, and United States and (West) Germany, Selected Periods, 1854–1969 46

A-2. U.K. Exports to the United States and U.S. Exports to the United Kingdom, 1951–1973 48

A-3. Canadian Exports to the United States and U.S. Exports to Canada, 1950–1972 49

A-4. Japanese Exports to the United States and U.S. Exports to Japan, 1950–1973 50

A-5. W. German Exports to the United States and U.S. Exports to W. Germany, 1952–1974 51

BUSINESS CYCLES IN THE POSTWAR WORLD

INTRODUCTION AND SUMMARY

One long-standing tenet of conventional economic wisdom is that business cycles in the United States tend to be transmitted inexorably and with an increase in severity to other market economies: when the United States sneezes, Europe catches cold. However, this study, albeit tentative and lacking detail, strongly suggests that no such simplistic explanation is sufficient. In the period after World War II, business-cycle peaks have generally occurred in other major industrialized economies before they have occurred in the United States: Europe has caught its colds before the United States has sneezed. (For business-cycle troughs, the order of precedence is mixed, with troughs in the U.S. economy preceding comparable foreign troughs as often as not.)

Actually, economists now distinguish two kinds of business cycles. The first is the familiar "classical" cycle with its booms and busts or (in the sterilized language of modern social scientists) expansions and recessions. The second—and at least during the post-World-War-II period, the more frequent—kind consists of cyclical variations in the rates of economic growth. Identification of these growth cycles is of extreme importance if we are to analyze the international transmission of cyclical instability, but appropriate procedures for identifying growth cycles are only now in process of being established.

This study reports on an investigation of whether the procedures used to identify classical cycles in the United States can also be used to identify growth cycles both in the United States and abroad. The evidence suggests that they can be. Moreover, reliable leading,

1

lagging, and coincident indicators appear to exist in foreign countries just as they do in the United States, and the timing classification of these indicators is the same elsewhere as it is in the United States. The study uses these indicators in examining the "sneeze hypothesis" and suggests that the reports of the contagion are greatly exaggerated.

I. CLASSICAL CYCLES

In 1967 some thirty-eight experts representing fourteen different countries gathered in London to debate the question, *Is the Business Cycle Obsolete?* Such is the power of the immediate past that the long expansion of the 1960s had made the topic seem distinctly relevant when the conference was originally planned. Of course one might have argued then that five or ten years of expansion did not make up a sufficiently long experience for us to write off a phenomenon that had been as persistent as the business cycle. In any case, by the time the conference's deliberations appeared in print—some two years later—there was substantial weakening at least in the U.S. economy, and the American participants in the London conference were forced to reconsider the question whether or when the United States had slipped into recession. Eventually we came to view the period from the end of 1969 to the end of 1970 as a recession.[1]

Still, the recession of 1969–1970 was fairly mild by almost all the measures economists use to measure recessions and optimists held to the view that even if expansion were not the unbroken wave of the future, at least it could be taken as the norm. By 1975, however, it was clear that the U.S. economy was suffering its most severe recession since World War II. During the course of the recession, in fact, some in the public press had discussed the possibility of another Great Depression. Although this possibility was dismissed by most economists, the mere fact that the question was raised is indicative of the change in attitudes toward business cycles during the past decade, away from the optimism of the mid-1960s.

With the customary benefit of hindsight we see now that America's "longest peacetime expansion"—from 1961 to 1969—was influ-

The author wishes to thank Gottfried Haberler, Geoffrey H. Moore, Ilse Mintz, Thomas F. Johnson, Dan Larkins, and Elizabeth Griffith for their helpful comments on an earlier draft of this paper. Responsibility for any remaining deficiencies is, of course, the author's.

[1] The record of the London Conference has been published in Martin Bronfenbrenner, ed., *Is the Business Cycle Obsolete?* (New York: Wiley-Interscience, 1969).

enced greatly by the redefinition of the term "peacetime" to include the Vietnam War and the increase in defense spending from $50 billion in fiscal year 1965 to $80 billion in fiscal year 1968 (current dollars). After the Great Depression, full employment was not restored until the United States entered World War II. The efficacy of military expenditures in eliminating recession has, therefore, been widely recognized, and did not really need the corroboration of the 1960s. (It seems likely that without the investment generated by the Vietnam War, the visible weakening of a number of economic indicators in 1965 would have signaled the onset of a mild recession, ending our "longest peacetime expansion.")

Another factor that seriously affected our view of instability was the lack of widespread price declines in postwar recessions. The tendency of inflation to persist during economic contraction has been widely observed, and has led economists to stress the measurement and study of real magnitudes of decline separately from magnitudes expressed in current prices. In times of increasingly severe inflation, real declines may be more than offset, and hence may be obscured, by increases in price levels. Indeed, the behavior of prices and real economic activity during a period of "stagflation" leads to one of the most vexing policy challenges we face. (Further compounding our recent policy difficulties, of course, has been the fact that both the price explosion of 1973—in large part influenced by the oil crisis— and the rapid deepening of the recession in the last quarter of 1974 were almost wholly unforeseen.)

One further aspect of recent cyclical experience deserves mention: rapid inflation has been experienced more or less in tandem by many industrial economies. This has caused some observers to argue that business cycles in the modern world have been more synchronous than they were earlier in this century, although it has always been possible for instability to be transmitted from country to country, so that domestic cycles would be aggravated, rather than mitigated, by overseas influences. The Great Depression is a classic example of how instability can spread to most of the market-oriented world. Research is needed to determine whether the cyclical movements of industrial economies have become more synchronous than they were and whether, as a result, small domestic disturbances are more likely than in the past to have important international consequences. There have been a number of previous periods of synchronous behavior (these are discussed below), and despite the breakdown of the gold standard (which tied countries together) and the introduction of floating exchange rates (designed to make countries more independent), there are factors that have increased the interdependence among the world's industrial economies.

The National Bureau's Point of Departure. The National Bureau of Economic Research (NBER)—the private research organization that pioneered the study of business cycles in the United States and that developed the major technique now used in this country to date business-cycle turning points—decided in 1973 that there was a need to broaden the focus of its cyclical research and study the business cycle in all major industrial countries. As a result, the NBER launched a project to develop international economic indicators—a project that could help all the countries involved tackle their common problems together.

It is worth recalling the widely quoted definition of business cycles that has served to guide the studies of the National Bureau in this field almost from its inception:

> Business cycles are a type of fluctuation found in the aggregate activity of nations that organize their work mainly in business enterprises; a cycle consists of expansions occurring at about the same time in many economic activities, followed by similarly general recessions, contractions, and revivals which merge into the expansion phase of the next cycle; this sequence of changes is recurrent but not periodic; in duration business cycles vary from more than one year to ten or twelve years; they are not divisible into shorter cycles of similar character with amplitudes approximating their own.[2]

Nowhere in this definition is there any suggestion that this kind of business cycle is peculiar to the United States. Indeed, one of the first publications of the National Bureau was Willard Thorp's *Business Annals*, which developed what we would now call business-cycle chronologies, albeit fairly crude ones, for some eighteen countries.

The notion that these cycles are found in "nations that organize their work mainly in business enterprises" might imply, of course, that the larger the percentage of a country's GNP produced by business enterprises (or the greater a country's devotion to the preservation of business enterprises), the more likely the presence of these business cycles might be. And, to be sure, just as the United States

[2] This definition, a modified version of the definition originally produced by Wesley Clair Mitchell in *Business Cycles: The Problem and Its Setting* (New York: National Bureau of Economic Research, 1927) is from *Measuring Business Cycles*, the pioneering methodological work by Arthur F. Burns and Wesley Mitchell (New York: National Bureau of Economic Research, 1947). (See p. 2.)

4

is outstanding among industrial countries in its efforts to maintain unfettered or minimally fettered business enterprises, so there is in fact some evidence that the United States has had more cycles than most other market-oriented economies, and that its cycles have been more severe than theirs. But it is not clear just why this has been the case, and the question has not been the subject of much careful analysis. Devotion to the preservation of business enterprises seems too simplistic an explanation: certainly it lacks rigor.

Much of the business-cycle work of the National Bureau has concentrated on refining the original technique used to date turning points in U.S. business cycles and on developing the forecasting possibilities inherent in the notion of leading indicators. In fact, the Bureau has become well known for its list of reliable leading indicators, as well as for its identification of a group of roughly coincident indicators and a group of lagging indicators.

As more data have become available, as knowledge has grown, as analyses have become more sophisticated, these lists of indicators have been revised several times. The first list, the work of Burns and Mitchell, was published in 1938. In 1950, this list was revised by Geoffrey H. Moore, the economist at the National Bureau most closely associated with continuing the work of Burns and Mitchell during the past quarter-century. The 1950 list was revised by Moore in 1960 and by Moore and Julius Shiskin in 1966.[3]

The 1966 revision produced a number of significant improvements. First, the indicators were divided into a short list of twenty-six "most reliable" indicators and a longer list of eighty-eight "reasonably reliable" indicators. Second, indicators were cross-classified by cyclical timing and economic process, the processes distinguished being those that are of major concern in the generation of business cycles. Finally, a technique was developed for scoring the indicators. This technique rated the indicators on the basis of such useful characteristics as economic significance, statistical adequacy of the underlying data, regularity with which the indicator conforms to the observed business cycles (as opposed to exhibiting what have come to be called "skipped" cycles or "extra" cyclical episodes of its own), consistency with which the series exhibits its overall timing relationship (leading, lagging, or

---

[3] See Wesley C. Mitchell and Arthur F. Burns, *Statistical Indicators of Cyclical Revivals*, Bulletin no. 69 (New York: National Bureau of Economic Research, 28 May 1938); Geoffrey H. Moore, *Statistical Indicators of Cyclical Revivals and Recessions*, Occasional Paper 31 (New York: National Bureau of Economic Research, 1950), reprinted in *Business Cycle Indicators* (G. H. Moore, ed.) chapter 7, pp. 184-260; and Julius Shiskin, *Indicators of Business Expansions and Contractions*, Occasional Paper 103 (New York: Columbia University Press for National Bureau of Economic Research, 1967).

roughly coincident) with U.S. business cycles at individual cyclical turning points, currency (the rapidity with which the series becomes available for use), and smoothness (the more volatile the series, the less likely that recent changes can be relied upon to reflect genuine cyclical movements).

In 1975, the Bureau of Economic Analysis published the most recent revision of the indicators, by Victor Zarnowitz and Charlotte Boschan. This revision not only altered the composition of the list of indicators, but also slightly revised some business-cycle turning points. Moreover, it differentiated real indicators from those measured in current prices, to facilitate forecasting in a period of rapid inflation. This is both valuable and important, for the reasons noted earlier.[4]

In all this revision and analysis of indicators, only rarely have timing classifications been changed. Revisions have customarily been made because, as more data have become available, new and better indicators (by the criteria enumerated above) could be substituted for older ones. Changes in the list cannot be interpreted as suggesting that the timing relationships are temporally capricious. Nor does the fact that indicators are more or less constantly under review mean that the "cycle" being forecast by the indicators is ephemeral or constantly changing. There is, of course, an element of secular change in most economic entities and the cycle is no exception. The recent emphasis on growth cycles as opposed to classical cycles is a good indication of such a change. But studies growing out of the work at the National Bureau suggest just how enduring have been many of the characteristics of business cycles.

A Current Perspective. In 1968, Arthur F. Burns surveyed the long history of economic instability and concluded that business cycles could be documented in the major industrialized market-oriented economies (the United States, Germany, France, and the United Kingdom) for quite long periods of time. In the case of the United Kingdom, in fact, cycles could be traced back to 1792. (See Table 1.) Although the chronology for the foreign countries ended in the 1930s, Burns noted that recent cyclical episodes had tended to be somewhat milder, reflecting perhaps what we had learned about controlling instability. Addressing himself to the possible obsolescence of the business cycle—a question that was being considered at the London conference (mentioned earlier) about the same time he was writing in the United States—Burns said it would "be premature to conclude that

---

[4] See U.S. Department of Commerce, *Business Conditions Digest*, May 1975, for details.

the older hazards of the business cycle belong to the past." [5] He went on to say it was "possible that in the future a 'recession' will mean merely a reduced rate of growth of aggregate economic activity instead of an actual and sustained decline, but there is as yet insufficient ground for believing that economic developments will generally conform to this model in the near future." [6] Thus, Burns fully appreciated the significance and durability of the pattern revealed by Table 1. Viewed from an historical perspective, the question whether business cycles as we had known them in the past were becoming obsolete was likely to prove premature, even in light of an eight- or ten-year expansion and even in a peacetime less equivocal than the United States experienced in the 1960s.

Burns did note, however, that in the postwar period many industrialized market-oriented economies grew rapidly and that business fluctuations were often relatively mild. Fluctuations in economic activity occasionally showed up as absolute changes in GNP (nominal or real) but customarily as deviations from the rising trend in GNP: they were reflected in various measures of economic activity including capacity utilization and unemployment rates. The way we measure trends (and the way we treat them after they are measured) has often crucially affected our ability to see—let alone measure—business fluctuations since World War II. The pre-World-War-II cycle, on the other hand, was usually much more severe than the postwar cycle, so that the elimination of trend (or even the failure to eliminate trend) in the earlier period had a smaller effect on the precise timing of turning points and other aspects of cyclical experience.

These secular and cyclical changes since World War II suggest that we refer to "classical cycles" as periods of absolute expansion and contraction, visible even without removing the trend from the time series being observed, while the term "growth cycle" more appropriately describes many postwar cycles that can be detected only as deviations about rising trends and can, therefore, be measured and analyzed only from trend-adjusted time series. Of course, none of this discussion should be taken to mean that classical cycles are exclusively pre-World-War-II phenomena and growth cycles exclusively postwar phenomena. Growth cycles (that is, cycles so mild as to be detected only in trend-adjusted data) did occur before the war,

---

[5] Arthur F. Burns, "The Nature and Causes of Business Cycles," *International Encyclopedia of the Social Sciences* (New York: Crowell-Collier and Macmillan, 1968). Reprinted in A. F. Burns, *The Business Cycle in a Changing World*, Studies in Business Cycles, no. 18 (New York: Columbia University Press for National Bureau of Economic Research, 1969), p. 50.

[6] Ibid., p. 50.

Table 1
CLASSICAL-CYCLE TURNING POINTS IN FOUR COUNTRIES, 1792–1961

United States		Great Britain	
Peak	**Trough**	**Peak**	**Trough**
	1834	1792	1793
1836	1838	1796	1797
1839	1843	1802	1803
1845	1846	1806	1808
1847	1848	1810	1811
1853	Dec. 1854	1815	1816
June 1857	Dec. 1858	1818	1819
Oct. 1860	June 1861	1825	1826
Apr. 1865	Dec. 1867	1828	1829
June 1869	Dec. 1870	1831	1832
Oct. 1873	Mar. 1879	1836	1837
Mar. 1882	May 1885	1839	1842
Mar. 1887	Apr. 1888	1845	1848
July 1890	May 1891	1854	Dec. 1854
Jan. 1893	June 1894	Sept. 1857	Sept. 1858
Dec. 1895	June 1897	Sept. 1860	Dec. 1862
June 1899	Dec. 1900	Mar. 1866	Mar. 1868
Sept. 1902	Aug. 1904	Sept. 1872	June 1879
May 1907	June 1908	Dec. 1882	June 1886
Jan. 1910	Jan. 1912	Sept. 1890	Feb. 1895
Jan. 1913	Dec. 1914	June 1900	Sept. 1901
Aug. 1918	Mar. 1919	June 1903	Nov. 1904
Jan. 1920	July 1921	June 1907	Nov. 1908
May 1923	July 1924	Dec. 1912	Sept. 1914
Oct. 1926	Nov. 1927	Oct. 1918	Apr. 1919
Aug. 1929	Mar. 1933	Mar. 1920	June 1921
May 1937	June 1938	Nov. 1924	July 1926
Feb. 1945	Oct. 1945	Mar. 1927	Sept. 1928
Nov. 1948	Oct. 1949	July 1929	Aug. 1932
July 1953	Aug. 1954	Sept. 1937	Sept. 1938
July 1957	Apr. 1958		
May 1960	Feb. 1961		

Source: Arthur F. Burns, *The Business Cycle in a Changing World* (New York: Columbia University Press for the NBER, 1969), Table 1.1, pp. 16-17.

but the violence of many cycles in that period makes such adjustment less crucial than it is for the postwar years. On the other hand, some postwar cyclical episodes, most notably the contraction in 1973–75, have been severe enough to be visible even in series unadjusted for trend. Certainly, therefore, both growth cycles and classical cycles warrant continued monitoring and analysis.

Business-cycle severity is frequently gauged by comparing the duration, depth, and diffusion of various cyclical episodes. Recently

	Germany			France		
	Peak		Trough	Peak		Trough
			1866			1840
	1869		1870	1847		1849
	1872	Feb.	1879	1853		1854
Jan.	1882	Aug.	1886	1857		1858
Jan.	1890	Feb.	1895	1864	Dec.	1865
Mar.	1900	Mar.	1902	Nov. 1867	Oct.	1868
Aug.	1903	Feb.	1905	Aug. 1870	Feb.	1872
July	1907	Dec.	1908	Sept. 1873	Aug.	1876
Apr.	1913	Aug.	1914	Apr. 1878	Sept.	1879
June	1918	June	1919	Dec. 1881	Aug.	1887
May	1922	Nov.	1923	Jan. 1891	Jan.	1895
Mar.	1925	Mar.	1926	Mar. 1900	Sept.	1902
Apr.	1929	Aug.	1932	May 1903	Oct.	1904
				July 1907	Feb.	1909
				June 1913	Aug.	1914
				June 1918	Apr.	1919
				Sept. 1920	July	1921
				Oct. 1924	June	1925
				Oct. 1926	June	1927
				Mar. 1930	July	1932
				July 1933	Apr.	1935
				June 1937	Aug.	1938

Geoffrey H. Moore examined the recession which began in late 1973, according to these three criteria. He compared the 1973–1975 recession with the most severe previous recession in the postwar period, 1957–1958, and with the two recessions of the 1929–1939 decade. (See Table 2.) The 1929–1933 decline was, of course, both the longest and the deepest of U.S. depressions in the twentieth century; the 1937–1938 decline was notable for the depth of decline, though it was of fairly brief duration.

Table 2
THE 1973–1975 CONTRACTION COMPARED WITH THREE PRECEDING CONTRACTIONS

| | 1973–75 | | | 1929–33 | |
	Based on available figures to date [a] (1)	1957–58 Full decline (2)	1937–38 Full decline (3)	Full decline (4)	Initial decline corresponding to (1) (5)
Duration (in months)					
Business cycle chronology	n.a.	9	13	43	n.a.
GNP, current $	3	6	9	42	3
GNP, constant $	15	6	6	36	15
Industrial production	18	14	12	36	18
Nonfarm employment	6	14	11	43	6
Unemployment rate	19	16	11	60[b]	18[d]
Depth (in percent)[c]					
GNP, current $	−1.0	−2.6	−16.2	−49.6	−2.5
GNP, constant $	−7.8	−3.9	−13.2	−32.6	−14.3
Industrial production	−14.0	−14.3	−32.4	−53.4	−30.0
Nonfarm employment	−3.2	−4.3	−10.8	−31.6	−5.0
Unemployment rate					
Low	4.6	3.7	11.0	3.2[b]	3.2[b]
High	9.2	7.5	20.0	25.2[b]	12.6[d]
Increase	+4.6	+3.8	+9.0	+22.0	+9.4
Diffusion					
Nonfarm industries: Maximum percentage with declining employment[e]	90 Jan. 1975	88 Sept. 1957	97 Dec. 1937	100 June 1933	100 Aug. 1930[f]

n.a. = not avaliable or not applicable.

[a] The intervals from peak to the lowest point reached to date are: GNP in constant dollars, Fourth Quarter 1973-First Quarter 1975; industrial production, November 1973-May 1975; nonfarm employment, October 1974-April 1975; unemployment rate, October 1973-May 1975.

[b] Based on annual averages for 1929 (low) and 1933 (high).

[c] Percentage change from the series' peak month or quarter to its trough month or quarter, over the intervals shown above.

[d] In lieu of monthly data, an estimate of the approximate unemployment rate eighteen months after the 1929 low (3.2 percent) was obtained by averaging the annual figures for 1930 and 1931 (8.9 and 16.3 percent respectively).

[e] For 1957-1958 and 1973-1975, based on changes in employment over six-month spans in thirty nonfarm industries, centered on the fourth month of the span. Hence the interval covered runs from three months before to three months after the month shown on the bottom line. For 1929-1933 and 1937-1938, based on cyclical changes in employment in forty-one industries.

[f] October 1930 is the date selected to correspond with January 1975 (col. 1), since both are fourteen months after the business cycle peak (August 1929 and November 1973, respectively).

Source: G. H. Moore, "Slowdowns, Recessions and Inflation," *Explorations in Economic Research,* vol. 2, no. 1, Spring 1975, Table 12, updated July 1975.

In assessing the evidence of Table 2, it is well to remember that the recession of the mid-1970s had not yet run its course when Moore made his calculations, although the table has here been updated to July 1975, at which point evidence had accumulated that the end of the recession was likely at hand. The comparison may nonetheless understate the ultimate magnitude of the decline in one or all of the dimensions included. November 1973 had been widely mentioned as a reasonable date for the onset of the recession, and was ultimately officially selected by the NBER as the date of onset. At present (July 1975) the trough of the recession has not been dated, since turning point determination must always await a good deal of confirming evidence. Moore coped with this difficulty by measuring the decline for each indicator from its own peak to the lowest point reached to date.

In duration, Moore's analysis suggests that the 1973–1975 recession was more severe than the 1957–1958 recession by all the measures except nonfarm employment (which had fallen for only six months) and GNP in current prices (which reflected the secular inflation that continued to plague the economy). In depth, the 1973–1975 recession was approximately comparable to the 1957–1958 recession as measured by the decline in industrial production, somewhat less severe as measured by the fall in nonfarm employment, and considerably more severe as measured by the fall in real GNP and the level of and increase in the unemployment rate. Finally, in diffusion, the recession of the mid-1970s approximated the severity of the 1957–1958 recession.

As the recession of the 1970s worsened, many of those affected asked whether it was likely to augur a return to the cyclical pattern of the interwar years. (This represented a sharp change from the "Is the business cycle obsolete?" query of the late 1960s.) Columns 4 and 5 of Table 2 provide evidence suggesting that the recession of the mid-1970s was much less severe than the Great Depression, according to almost all criteria. And column 3 suggests that while the decline of the 1970s surpassed the duration of the 1937–1938 decline as shown in most of the available indicators, the depth and diffusion of the recession were both still a good deal less severe than for the 1937–1938 recession.

In general we may conclude that the recession of the mid-1970s was probably about one-fourth as severe as the Great Depression, perhaps one-half as severe as the 1937–1938 recession and, depending on the measures compared, equal to or slightly worse than the 1957–1958 recession. (A striking difference among these recessions, of course, involves the behavior of prices; prices have been much less flexible in post-World-War-II recessions than they were in earlier declines. Nonetheless, an abatement in the rate of inflation was evident by early 1975.) As the next section indicates, the need for new ways of examining instability has become widely recognized. But this should not blind us to the continued need to monitor instability in the ways found useful in the past.

II. GROWTH CYCLES: NEW WINE OR NEW BOTTLES?

Several years ago Geoffrey H. Moore described what has come to be known as the "growth cycle" view of business fluctuations as "both old and new." [1] He pointed out that the notion was somewhat akin to Arthur Burns's view of the "unseen cycle" which (in contrast to the "seen" expansions and contractions in aggregate economic activity) takes form in the distribution of expansions and contractions within aggregate economic activity. We have already noted Burns's suggestion that growth cycles might become important in the future. Moore pointed out that as much as forty years before Burns discussed the "unseen cycle" in the National Bureau's Annual Report for 1950, economists like Henry L. Moore, Warren Persons, Frederick Macaulay, and Edwin Frickey had considered whether cycles might appear as shorter recurring movements about long-term trends.[2]

The Rediscovery of the Growth Cycle. The concern with variations in rates of growth died out until after the Second World War, but in the 1950s, as R. A. Gordon has noted, economists such as Burns, Brinley Thomas, Moses Abramowitz, and Simon Kuznets became interested in these variations once again. The movements came to be known as Kuznets cycles and Gordon defined them as "alternations in the *rate of growth,* not in the absolute magnitudes, of such variables as output, population and the labor force, the supply of money, the stock of capital, productivity, and so on." [3]

A major difference between Kuznets cycles and modern growth cycles, however, is that the former were regarded as averaging about

[1] Geoffrey H. Moore, Foreword to Ilse Mintz, *Dating Postwar Business Cycles* (New York: Columbia University Press for National Bureau of Economic Research, 1969), p. xi.

[2] These early efforts are considered in Mitchell, *Business Cycles: The Problem and its Setting,* pp. 190-233. Burns and Mitchell also directed attention to this technique in *Measuring Business Cycles.*

[3] See R. A. Gordon, *Business Fluctuations,* 2d ed. (New York: Harper & Row, 1961), pp. 241-243. Italics in original.

twenty years in duration, whereas the latter are much shorter. Like Kuznets cycles, growth cycles involve fluctuations in the intensity with which capacity is employed rather than fluctuations in the growth of capacity. In this regard, determination of the modern growth cycle, like the determination of the classical cycle, should facilitate analysis of the tendency for modern market-oriented economies to deviate from their full-employment growth potential on a recurring basis. This was, of course, the question to which the Council of Economic Advisers originally directed the attention of economists in the early 1960s and it is reflected in continuing concern with the "GNP gap." [4]

For practical reasons, economists became interested in growth cycles after World War II, because for some years—especially abroad—there was very little evidence for the continued existence of classical cycles. There were classical cycles in the United States but, as already noted, they were mild. West Germany did not experience any classical cycles in the post-World-War-II period until 1966–1967, when there was a clear contraction in German economic activity.[5] Much the same thing was true of Britain's postwar history. R.C.O. Matthews noted in the late 1960s that "in no postwar year has there been a significant decline in real gross domestic product (GDP). Fluctuations have taken the form of oscillations in the growth rate." [6] While there was evidence of considerable instability in Japan during the postwar years, despite the remarkably rapid rate of growth there, it is fair to say that in general all the industrialized market-oriented countries exhibited the same kind of behavior as West Germany and the United Kingdom.

In the mid-1960s economists frequently argued that we had learned enough about instability so that macroeconomic policy could keep recessions within the relatively mild bounds characterized by our more recent cycles. Accordingly, attention moved to the possibilities of studying growth cycles in the U.S. economy. At the National Bureau the interest in growth cycles produced studies on several fronts. The first to see the published light of day was Ilse Mintz's study of postwar growth cycles in the United States, the methodology

[4] An extended debate concerning the relevance as well as the techniques of measuring the GNP gap, involving Arthur F. Burns and the Kennedy Council of Economic Advisers, appeared in the *Morgan Guaranty Survey* (New York: Morgan Guaranty Trust Company, May and August, 1961).

[5] Mintz, *Dating Postwar Business Cycles*, pp. 44-46.

[6] R.C.O. Matthews, "Postwar Business Cycles in the United Kingdom" in *Is the Business Cycle Obsolete?* ed. M. Bronfenbrenner, p. 99.

of which essentially duplicated her methodology in studying such cycles in West Germany.[7]

As was the case with her study of West Germany, Mrs. Mintz confined her attention largely to the "roughly coincident" indicators previously identified in NBER business-cycle research. Concentrating on these important and widely used indicators of aggregate economic activity, she devoted her work to two methods of dating growth-cycle turns. The first method employed deviations from longer-term trends and the second, adapted from earlier work by Milton Friedman and Anna Schwartz, employed what have come to be known as "step-cycles." Both techniques yielded essentially similar results. Her findings, set out in Table 3, show that there was a growth-cycle turning point corresponding to each of the nine classical-cycle turning points for the United States during the period 1948–1969 (the classical-cycle turning points being determined by conventional NBER methods). Her growth-cycle turns differed by no more than five months from the classical-cycle turns, with the growth-cycle peaks leading the classical-cycle peaks and the growth-cycle troughs coincident with or lagging the classical-cycle troughs. These differences are to be expected in comparing the turning points between trend-adjusted and unadjusted series. In addition to the growth cycles which corresponded with all the recorded classical cycles in the United States during this period, however, she recorded an extra growth cycle covering the Korean War period, 1951–1952, and two extra growth cycles during the "long expansion" of the 1960s—one in 1962–1963, and the other in 1966–1967.[8]

On another active front, the National Bureau launched a study of International Economic Indicators (IEI) in 1973. This project was tied closely to the increased emphasis on growth cycles. It has already been noted that the United States had more classical cycles than other countries in the postwar period. Early evidence, however, led to the suspicion that the degree of correspondence among growth cycles in various market-oriented economies might be considerably greater than the degree of correspondence among classical cycles. Specifically there were indications that each of the three "growth recessions"

---

[7] Her results are published as "Dating United States Growth Cycles" in *Explorations in Economic Research*, vol. 1, no. 1, Summer 1974, pp. 1-113. A preliminary version is published in *The Business Cycle Today*, Victor Zarnowitz, ed., 50th Anniversary Colloquium, vol. 1 (New York: Columbia University Press for NBER, 1972).

[8] For a different way of viewing the cyclical episodes during this period, see John R. Meyer and Daniel H. Weinberg, "On the Classification of Economic Fluctuations" in *Explorations in Economic Research*, vol. 2, no. 2, Spring 1975.

Table 3

COMPARISON OF GROWTH-CYCLE AND CLASSICAL-CYCLE
TURNING POINTS, UNITED STATES, 1948–1970

Dates of Peaks			Dates of Troughs		
Growth cycles	Classical cycles	Lead (−) or lag (+) (in months) [a]	Growth cycles	Classical cycles	Lead (−) or lag (+) (in months)
8/48	11/48	−3	11/49	10/49	+1
5/51	—	—	7/52	—	—
3/53	7/53	−4	9/54	8/54	+1
2/57	7/57	−5 [b]	5/58	4/58	+1
2/60	5/60	−3 [b]	2/61	2/61	0
4/62	—	—	4/63	—	—
6/66	—	—	10/67	—	—
6/69	11/69	−5 [b]	n.a.	11/70	n.a.
Average lead (−) or lag (+)		−4			+.8

[a] Month turns are compared to classical turns.
[b] Revised.

Sources: Growth cycles—Ilse Mintz, "Dating United States Growth Cycles" in *Explorations in Economic Research,* vol. 1, no. 1, p. 59; classical cycles—*Business Conditions Digest,* U.S. Department of Commerce, Bureau of Economic Analysis (Washington, D. C., Monthly Report).

which did not correspond to classical recessions in the United States were matched by similar occurrences in the United Kingdom and West Germany.

The IEI project was designed to explore the possibility of developing a growth-cycle chronology of turning points for each of the major industrialized market-oriented economies for which the necessary data could be acquired. This effort in a sense could be viewed as another step in broadening the scope of NBER work to cover the "economies that organize their work mainly in business enterprises," in the words of Burns and Mitchell in 1946. The years since their definition of business cycles appeared had been largely devoted to the task of measuring cycles in the United States, although the studies by Mintz, Morgenstern, Michaely, and Friedman and Schwartz had in part redressed the balance toward concern with what was happening outside our national boundaries. The time had certainly come for broadening an unduly parochial emphasis on our own economy, however necessary the emphasis had been in forging the tools and developing the techniques required in studying business fluctuations in the industrialized market-oriented world.

In addition to including more national economies in its range, the IEI project broadened the focus in several other ways. Ilse Mintz had in a real sense been a pioneer in developing feasible techniques for dating growth cycles in enterprise economies. But she had paid relatively little attention to the development of German equivalents for those leading and lagging indicators of cyclical activity which have been useful in the United States, both in forecasting and in the analysis necessarily preceding policy initiatives.[9] Attempts to relate the whole range of indicators developed in the United States to cycles in other industrialized enterprise economies truly opened the way to new possibilities in research. In effect the attempt was being made to forge a new tool with which to study the interrelations among economic fluctuations in different countries, both currently and historically. A number of crucial questions were being asked: What variables should be watched to detect promptly those retardations in growth or accelerations in economic activity (both real and monetary) that become widespread internationally? How do booms and recessions which become worldwide in scope differ from those that do not? What economic processes, in which countries, are sensitive and what processes are relatively immune to worldwide changes in real growth rates or in inflation rates? How are the competitive relations among countries affected by shifts in these variables? What do the relationships of economic factors tell us about the transmission mechanisms of international disturbance? In particular, is there more transmission under fixed or under floating rates? Is it possible to learn anything about which countries and which sectors of their economies are most likely to contain the initiating impulse for those disturbances which travel to other sectors and other economies? And are there sectors and economies which rarely or never initiate international disturbances but instead invariably are passively acted on by other economies or sectors?

The answers to these questions should help us observe and explain the variations in the business cycle among countries at any

---

[9] The Germans themselves have customarily followed the common European tendency of relying on "qualitative indicators" in predicting future economic developments. The IFO-Institute in Munich has been particularly prominent in the development of these indicators, which rely on surveys of entrepreneurs and others to develop a consensus of anticipations about future economic developments. Increasingly, attention on both sides of the Atlantic is being focused upon combining qualitative and quantitative indicators in forecasting.

given time. Such observation and explanation could have important consequences for international monetary relations, exports and imports, capital flows, balance of payments, inflation rates, exchange rates and exchange stability, international investment in capital formation, comparative growth rates—and, in short, for knowing whether international economic relations can generally be expected to mitigate or only to exacerbate international tensions.

The International Economic Indicators project accordingly has directed its initial efforts towards developing for the more important or accessible enterprise economies a set of time series for other countries which could be termed rough equivalents to the twenty-six U.S. indicators of business cycles on the 1966 NBER "short list." These indicators were chosen as a convenient and useful—as well as a manageable—point of departure. They were augmented by series reflecting the international economic relations for each country. (Such series are absent from the U.S. short list only because international trade represents a small percentage of the U.S. GNP. This is not the case for most other countries and the potential usefulness of the international series will be illustrated below.) Finally, an effort was made to develop data on the behavior of time series that reflected cyclical developments in individual countries, even though these series had not been important in the United States. Not only was such information obviously necessary in considering cyclical indicators country by country, but it was hoped it would be of value worldwide to all who are concerned with international cyclical fluctuations.

The initial endeavors of the International Economic Indicators project showed that, as of 1973–1974, interest almost everywhere was concentrated on growth cycles. In most European economies, as well as in Japan, Australia, Canada and other market-oriented economies outside the United States, the evidence was overwhelming that business cycles were still manifestly present but often as uneven rates of growth (growth cycles) rather than as absolute changes in direction (classical cycles). There was, moreover, great interest expressed worldwide in utilizing National Bureau methods to study these growth cycles.

As the initial exploratory work continued, we became convinced that it would be feasible to develop chronologies of turning points in growth cycles in a number of countries—the data for this endeavor would indeed be forthcoming. The evidence that gradually emerged appeared to suggest that despite the general tendency of postwar cycles to take the form of recurring differential growth rates, the notion of reliable leading, coincident, and lagging indicators could be shown to have wide application in many countries outside the United States.

Ultimately, of course, the question that must be explored is whether the complex pattern of interrelationships reflected in growth cycles is simply a new manifestation of the interrelationships reflected historically in classical cycles, or whether it is a new phenomenon. While the question must perforce remain open for the time being, there is considerable evidence to suggest that we are dealing with a new manifestation of an old phenomenon. This likelihood that we are dealing with "old wine in a new bottle" is considered a bit further in the section to follow.

Is the Growth Cycle Obsolete? The question so posed is meant to be facetious. It is designed to suggest that we should have learned in the 1960s to be wary of ex cathedra pronouncements concerning fundamental and lasting changes in economic phenomena, particularly when those phenomena have been corroborated by evidence covering a long period of time. We should be especially wary when the change is supported by data which may cover only the recent past and which may therefore represent ephemeral conditions. If the quarter century following World War II was an inadequately brief period on which to predicate the obsolescence of the business cycle, the recession beginning in 1973 is certainly too recent and isolated an episode on which to predicate the unimportance of growth cycles. To be sure, no one (to our knowledge) has yet chosen to declare the passing of growth cycles from the scene. But there have been a number of suggestions, inferring from the severity attached to some measures of the recession of the mid-1970s, that the classical business cycle might not have been tamed after all.

We have previously alluded to some of the factors which have, in our judgment, caused the recession of the mid-1970s to be more severe than most or all of its post-World-War-II predecessors. We may note the increased power of concentrated units in the economy, a power that makes administered prices and cost-push inflation more likely and traditional wage-price flexibility correspondingly less likely than in earlier times.[10] We may note the inflationary impact of the

---

[10] I do not refer here to the old but continuing controversy concerning the nature of secular changes (if any) in concentration ratios. Rather I refer to the myriad discussions of corporate power and its relation to the growing absolute size of corporations, union power and its relation to the size of unions, and so on. I refer also to the frequently expressed view that there is an increasing likelihood (through administered prices and industry-wide collective bargaining) that wages and prices will be relatively inflexible. For detailed discussion of this, the

18

Vietnam War and the international implications of having severe inflations occur more or less simultaneously in a number of economies. Along with these features, which gave the recent past its distinctive character, there were also factors giving it continuity with the long history of business fluctuations covered in classical cycles. Conventional theory, for example, has long argued that the greater an inflationary boom, the greater would be the succeeding contraction.[11] Paradoxically, therefore, the very magnitude of the real growth rate which was so impressive as to cause many in the 1960s and early 1970s to argue that classical declines were a thing of the past (or at least less likely to occur than in the past) would have caused traditional theorists to predict just such a relatively severe decline as many of the world's industrialized economies in fact experienced in the mid-1970s.

There were twenty-six business cycles in the United States between 1854 and 1961, of which twenty had expansions of thirty-six months or less—the length of the expansion from November 1970 to November 1973. This being the case, the onset of the recession in 1973 was historically already somewhat "overdue." If we restrict our attention to the period after World War II, we find that the average peacetime cyclical expansion in the years from 1945 to 1961 was precisely thirty-six months, thus suggesting (as one possible hy-

---

reader may consult, for example, Gardner Means, "The Administered Price Thesis Reconfirmed," *American Economic Review*, June 1972, pp. 292-306. The great power of large units in the American economy has been developed by many, most conspicuously in the recent writings of J. K. Galbraith. It is corroborated, for example, by Walter Adams, who commented in his testimony before the Select Committee on Small Business, 90th Congress, 1st sess., 1967 that "Galbraith's contention that corporate giantism dominates American industry requires no adumbration." Finally, Phillip Cagan has noted that the "prevalence of downward rigidity is widely assumed," in *The Hydra-Headed Monster* (Washington, D.C.: American Enterprise Institute, 1974), p. 37.

[11] This view is particularly associated with "psychological explanations" of the business cycle of the Pigovian variety. See, for example, the discussion of Pigou in James Estey's text of a few years ago. "The very magnitude of the boom, which is another way of saying the very magnitude of the optimistic error, tends to make an equally great excess of pessimism." James Estey, *Business Cycles*, 3rd ed. (Englewood Cliffs, New Jersey: Prentice Hall, Inc., 1956), p. 188.

More recently, monetarists have argued that wrong-headed intervention by the monetary authorities often exacerbates instability. The greater the stimulus, the more extreme the policy response and the consequent reversal in the cycle is correspondingly more extreme, producing "policy cycles." Milton Friedman characterizes much Federal Reserve policy in this way. For example, recessions in 1919-20, 1937-38, 1953-54, 1959-60 involved changes in growth in the money supply which caused him to argue, "Too late and too much has been the general practice." Milton Friedman, "The Role of Monetary Policy," *American Economic Review*, vol. 48, no. 1 (March 1958), p. 16. (This was Friedman's presidential address to the American Economic Association.)

Table 4

COMPARISON OF TURNING POINTS IN ALTERNATIVE GROWTH-CYCLE CHRONOLOGIES, UNITED STATES, 1948–1973

Dates of Upturns		Lead (−) or Lag (+)	Dates of Downturns		Lead (−) or Lag (+)
Unrestricted basis [a]	Restricted basis [a]	(in months)	Unrestricted basis [a]	Restricted basis [a]	(in months)
			8/48	7/48	−1
11/49	10/49	−1	5/51	6/61	+1
7/52	6/52	−1	3/53	3/53	0
9/54	8/54	−1	2/57	2/57	0
5/58	5/58	0	2/60	2/60	0
2/61	2/61	0	4/62	4/62	0
4/63	3/63	−1	6/66	6/66	0
10/67	10/67	0	6/69	3/69	−3
11/70 [b]	n.a.	—	11/73 [b]	n.a.	—

n.a. = not available.

[a] The unrestricted basis uses series expressed in current as well as in constant prices and in physical units. The restricted basis is limited to series in constant price and in physical units.

[b] Updated at the National Bureau for Economic Research.

Source: Ilse Mintz, "Dating United States Growth Cycles," *Explorations in Economic Research*, vol. 1, no. 1, p. 59.

pothesis) that the recession of 1973 was a "reversion to type" after the long expansion of the 1960s.

Each cyclical episode has elements which make it unique as well as elements which suggest that it is part of the long-run pattern of cyclical fluctuation. This long-run pattern has been sufficiently pronounced to justify continued efforts to develop both business-cycle theory and better techniques of cyclical measurement. In recent years it may well be that we have made more headway in developing better measurement techniques than we have in developing better theory. It may be that the changes which have suggested the addition of growth-cycle analysis to our previous classical analysis are simply too new to be well understood. In either case, the recent past neither suggests the obsolescence of previous classical business-cycle work done at the National Bureau and elsewhere, nor does it suggest that our present concern with growth cycles is inappropriate.

Developing Chronologies. As we noted earlier, Ilse Mintz has shown that the conventional coincident indicators of U.S. classical cycles can be used in a new way to identify growth cycles in the United States and in West Germany. Actually, Mintz developed two chronologies for the United States. One was based on consensus turning points in aggregates denominated in current prices, in constant prices, and in physical units; the other was restricted to consensus turning points in the second and third of these. The two chronologies are shown in Table 4. Note that in several cases turning points are actually shifted when we take account of the impact of inflation.

For the time being, we are continuing to identify turns by what Table 4 refers to as "the unrestricted basis" because we want to study in comparable fashion all the economies included in the International Economic Indicators program. While there are some relatively minor differences between turns chosen on the restricted basis and turns chosen on the unrestricted basis, the major change introduced by the switch to growth cycles is the addition of three cycles to the classical-cycle chronology. The long expansion of the 1960s is now interrupted by a recession in 1962–1963 and another in 1967–1968. The other newly marked recession occurred in 1951–1952 at the time of the Korean War.

It is important to bear in mind that the U.S. growth-cycle turns were selected by applying a new methodology to the coincident indicators previously identified in our work on classical cycles.[12] Table 5 below is instructive because it shows what happens to timing when we look at the same indicators, first from the perspective of the customary classical-cycle chronology and then from the perspective of the new (undeflated) growth-cycle chronology.

It would appear that the timing of these six indicators at classical turns does not differ radically from their timing at growth-cycle turning points. There are interesting differences for individual indicators—personal income and the unemployment rate are more closely attuned to growth-cycle turns than to classical-cycle turns, while the index of industrial production deviates slightly less from the classical-cycle turns than from the growth-cycle turns. However, the differences

---

[12] The NBER method for choosing growth-cycle turning points has been programmed for the computer. It involves selecting tentative turning points from the deviation from a 75-month moving average in each series. Final turns are obtained by allowing for the variations in the length of different growth-cycle phases by computing a three-phase moving average of the series, the phases being based on the tentatively selected turning points. It is the resulting cycles in individual series, representing alternating periods when the rate of growth was above and below its long-run trend, from which the growth-cycle turns are selected.

Table 5

TIMING COMPARISON OF SIX ROUGHLY COINCIDENT INDICATORS AT CLASSICAL-CYCLE AND GROWTH-CYCLE TURNING POINTS, UNITED STATES, 1948–1970

Roughly Coincident Indicators on U.S. "Short" List	Median Timing (in months)			
	Classical cycles		Growth cycles	
	Peaks	Troughs	Peaks	Troughs
1. Personal income	+1	−2	0	0
2. GNP, current prices (Q)	0	−1	+1	0
3. GNP, constant prices (Q)	0	−3	−0.5	−1
4. Index of industrial production	0	0	−0.5	−1
5. Employees on nonagricultural payrolls	−2	0	−0.5	+1
6. Unemployment rate (inverted) − %	−4	+2	0	0
Mean of medians	−0.8	−0.7	−0.1	−0.2
Median of medians	0	−0.5	−0.2	0

Sources: Classical cycles—Geoffrey H. Moore and Julius Shiskin, *Indicators of Business Expansions and Contractions,* Occasional Paper 103 (New York: Columbia University Press for NBER, 1967), App. B., col. 10, pp. 96-97; growth cycles—calculated from Ilse Mintz, "Dating United States Growth Cycles," *Explorations in Economic Research,* vol. 1, no. 1, Summer 1974, Table 11.

between the timing at growth-cycle turns and at classical-cycle turns are never larger than four months (the difference which shows up in unemployment at cyclical peaks). Moreover, classical cycles represent turns in original (seasonally adjusted) data, while growth cycles represent turns in trend-adjusted data. This difference in itself would produce some changes in the location of turning points. Thus we can safely conclude, on the evidence now available, that when all the indicators are analyzed at comparable growth-cycle turns it is unlikely that we shall find results significantly different from those already found.

The National Bureau's IEI program has thus far produced growth-cycle chronologies for the United Kingdom, Canada, Japan, and West Germany. For the United States, it is unlikely that there will be significant changes from the chronology previously developed

Figure 1

POSTWAR GROWTH-CYCLE CHRONOLOGIES OF FIVE COUNTRIES,
WITH LEADS (−) AND LAGS (+) VS. UNITED STATES

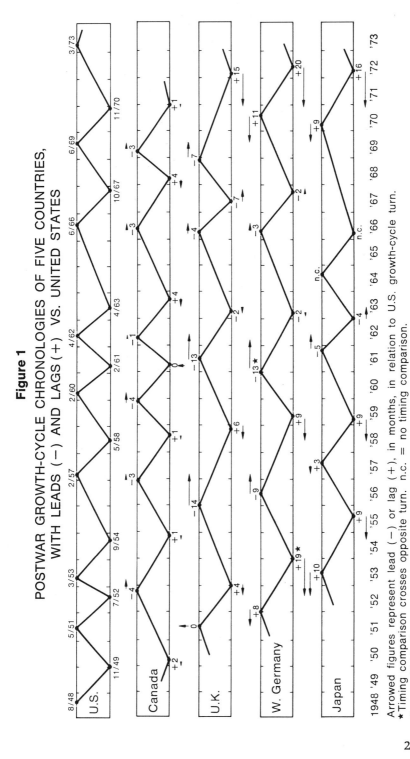

Arrowed figures represent lead (−) or lag (+), in months, in relation to U.S. growth-cycle turn.
★Timing comparison crosses opposite turn. n.c. = no timing comparison.
Source: Table 6.

23

Table 6

POSTWAR GROWTH-CYCLE CHRONOLOGIES FOR FIVE COUNTRIES WITH LEADS (−) AND LAGS (+) IN COMPARISON WITH THE UNITED STATES, 1948–1973

Peak	Trough	United States[a]	United Kingdom[b]	
P		8/48		
	T	11/49		
P		5/51	5/51 (0)	
	T	7/52		11/52 (+4)
P		3/53		
	T	9/54		
P		2/57	12/55 (−14)	
	T	5/58		11/58 (+6)
P		2/60		
	T	2/61		
P		4/62	3/61 (−13)	
	T	4/63		2/63 (−2)
P		6/66	2/66 (−4)	
	T	10/67		3/67 (−7)
P		6/69	11/68 (−7)	
	T	11/70[e]		2/72 (+15)
P		3/73[e]		
Summary				
Number of leads			4	2
Number of coincidences			1	0
Number of lags			0	3
Mean lead (−) or lag (+) in months			−7.6	−3.2

n.c. = no timing comparison.

[a] Ilse Mintz, "Dating United States Growth Cycles," *Explorations in Economic Research,* Summer 1974, p. 59.

[b] IEI Project, March 6, 1975.

[c] IEI Project, June 23, 1975. These dates differ somewhat from those derived by Ilse Mintz, *Dating Postwar Business Cycles: Methods and Their Application to Western Germany, 1950-67* (New York: Columbia University Press for NBER, 1969).

[d] Crosses opposite turn. The NBER rules for comparing cycle phases do not customarily permit the comparison of a trough (peak) in one series with a trough (peak) in another if there is an intervening peak (trough) in the series being compared with the referent series. We have made an exception here in the international comparisons.

[e] Updated at the National Bureau for Economic Research.

West Germany[c]		Japan[b]		Canada[b]	
					1/50 (+2)
1/52 (+8)					
	2/54 (+19)[d]				
		1/54 (+10)		11/52 (−4)	
			6/55 (+9)		10/54 (+1)
5/56 (−9)		5/57 (+3)		11/56 (−3)	
	2/59 (+9)		2/59 (+9)		6/58 (+1)
				10/59 (−4)	
					2/61 (0)
3/61 (−13)		11/61 (−5)		3/62 (−1)	
	2/63 (−2)		12/62 (−4)		8/63 (+4)
3/66 (−3)		8/64 (n.c.)		3/66 (−3)	
	8/67 (−2)		2/66 (n.c.)		2/68 (+4)
5/70 (+11)		3/70 (+9)		3/69 (−3)	
	7/72 (+20)		3/72 (+16)		12/70 (+1)
2/73 (−1)					
4	2	1	1	6	0
0	0	0	0	0	1
2	3	3	3	0	6
−1.2	+8.8	+4.2	+7.0	−3.0	+1.9

by Ilse Mintz.[13] The five chronologies can, therefore, be examined together as indicating what may be revealed in the development of growth-cycle chronologies in the postwar period in market-oriented economies. We have indicated the turning points in Table 6 and shown them schematically in Figure 1.

What can we conclude from this evidence? First of all, it is clear that the methodology developed at the NBER for measuring growth cycles in the United States may be adapted for use for other countries and that its origins in classical-cycle analysis do not impair its ability to delineate growth cycles. While much remains to be done both in refining our techniques and in extending the analysis to other countries, much seems to have been clarified already.

While all classical cycles will show up in growth-cycle chronologies (often, however, with dates changed somewhat by the introduction of trend-adjusted series from which turning points are selected), all growth cycles do not of course reflect classical cycles. Many countries will therefore exhibit more growth cycles than classical cycles. Precise comparisons are not possible, but West Germany, for example, is customarily viewed as having had only one classical recession after the war and before the 1970s (in 1966–1967). But Figure 1 shows clearly that West Germany experienced five growth recessions through 1972, one more than Mrs. Mintz was able to show in her chronology, which ended in 1967.

Figure 1 also shows that for the comparable period for all five countries, roughly 1952–1973, the United States and Canada had six growth recessions, while West Germany and Japan had five and the

---

[13] Indeed, since the NBER program has been employed in selecting turns for West Germany, they can be compared with Mintz's West German turns. The program, described in the previous footnote, differs from Mrs. Mintz's in that she selected final turns from a 75-month moving average. She also used a somewhat different set of coincident indicators. For purposes of comparison we present below both the National Bureau's West German chronology and Mrs. Mintz's.

Peaks		Troughs	
NBER	Mintz	NBER	Mintz
1/52	4/51 (−9)	2/54	1/54 (−1)
5/56	1/56 (−4)	2/59	3/59 (+1)
3/61	1/61 (−2)	2/63	2/63 (0)
3/66	12/65 (−3)	8/67	6/67 (−2)
5/70			
2/73		8/72	

Average lead (−) or   −4.5   −.5
Lag (+) in months

Similarly small differences can be expected when the NBER program selects a growth cycle chronology for the United States.

United Kingdom had four. In addition, the United States had one recession more than the United Kingdom in the early 1950s. Clearly the business cycle is not obsolete. For our purposes, in the next section, the most important point that emerges from the comparison of these growth-cycle chronologies has to do with the timing of the peaks and troughs. In both the table and the figure, the U.S. chronology has been used as a reference chronology and the leads(−) and lags(+) in months of the other comparable turns have been indicated. The pattern of these leads and lags—in other words, the timing of the peaks and troughs among countries—is the point at which we begin our discussion of the international transmission of instability.

III. THE INTERNATIONAL TRANSMISSION OF INSTABILITY

The most provocative question raised by Figure 1 and Table 6 concerns the leads and lags from the reference (U.S.) turns. The consistency with which the peaks in the U.S. chronology lag matching peaks in Canada, West Germany, and the United Kingdom is striking. In Japan, the peaks are more apt to lag and the troughs are mixed. The mean timing of the turning points in each country (as compared to the turning points in the United States) is shown in Table 6, both at peaks and at troughs. In all the countries except Japan, the foreign peaks typically lead U.S. peaks while the troughs frequently lag U.S. troughs. How is this to be interpreted?

The twenty-year period shown in Figure 1 should be put into historical perspective in order for us to determine whether this tendency of European growth-cycle turns to precede U.S. growth-cycle turns is something new, something unique to growth cycles, or simply the culmination of changes already underway in the relationship of cycles in the U.S. economy and the European economies. Figure 2 summarizes in schematic fashion the turning points in classical cycles for the United States, the United Kingdom, and Germany. (Prewar data are not available for Canada and Japan.) Table 7 shows the mean timing of the turning points for selected time periods, using the U.S. turns as the referent.

Let us consider the U.S.-U.K. comparison first. The traditional view that peaks in U.S. cycles precede peaks in U.K. cycles was consistent with the facts during the period from 1854 to 1938, but the U.K. lag in the interwar period was one month shorter on the average than the lag before World War I. So viewed, the fact that U.K. growth-cycle peaks stop lagging behind U.S. peaks in the post-

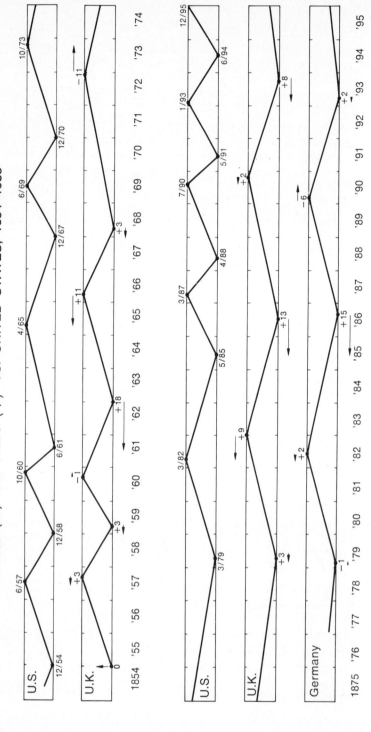

Figure 2

CLASSICAL-CYCLE CHRONOLOGIES OF THREE COUNTRIES, WITH LEADS (−) AND LAGS (+) VS. UNITED STATES, 1854–1938

Figure 2 (continued)

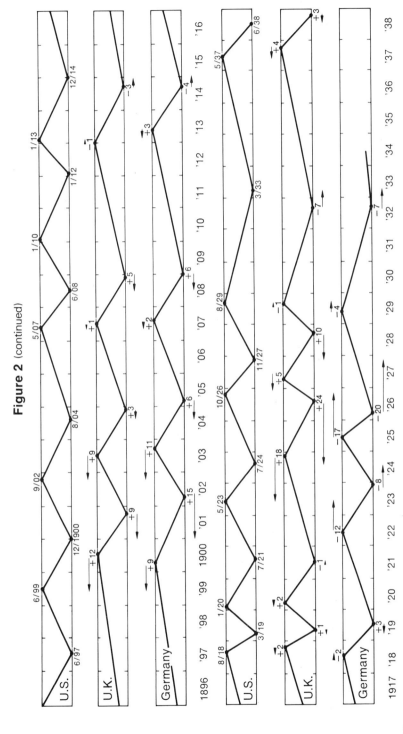

Table 7

COMPARISON OF MATCHED TURNS IN CYCLES, UNITED KINGDOM AND UNITED STATES, (W.) GERMANY AND UNITED STATES, WITH U.S. TURNS AS REFERENCE CHRONOLOGY, SELECTED PERIODS, 1854–1972

(figures in months)

	Peak	Trough	Peak and Trough
A. United Kingdom and United States			
Classical cycles			
1854–1938	+3.1	+4.2	+3.7
1854–1914	+3.4	+5.6	+4.6
1915–1938	+2.4	+1.2	+1.8
Growth cycles			
1950–1972	−7.6	+3.2	−1.5
B. (W.) Germany and United States			
Classical cycles			
1879–1938	+.3	+2.7	+1.6
1879–1914	+3.5	+5.6	+4.6
1915–1938	−6.0	−4.0	−5.0
Growth cycles			
1950–1968	−8.75	+5.5	−1.6

Note: Figures are the mean timing of all matched turns in each period.
Source: Table 1.

1952 period is merely the culmination of a long historical trend. In the post-World-War-II period the temporal relationship finally changed direction at the peaks, with the United Kingdom customarily (and for the first time) leading the United States at downturns. At troughs the relations have not reversed; the lag in U.K. troughs behind U.S. troughs is now shorter than in the earliest period, but slightly longer than in the interwar period. The lag at troughs is much shorter than the lead at peaks, however, with the result that the behavior at peaks and troughs combined produces on the average a lead for the United Kingdom in the post-World-War-II period, compared to the lags (successively shorter but still lags) that one finds in the period before World War II.[1]

Comparisons between West Germany (all Germany before World War II) and the United States are for a more limited period of time

---

[1] The details of the United States-United Kingdom and United States-West German turning point comparisons are shown in Table A-1.

but produce somewhat similar results. There was a short lag of German peaks behind U.S. peaks in the period 1879–1914, a lead in the interwar period, and a longer lead at growth-cycle peaks in the period after World War II. This repeats the pattern of secular change found in the relationship between U.K. and U.S. peaks, except that German peaks led U.S. peaks before World War II. At troughs there is no clear pattern. German troughs lag behind U.S. troughs both in the earliest period and recently, but lead in the interwar period. However ambiguous the U.S.-(West) German comparison may be at troughs, the evidence is clear at peaks and, as with the comparison of U.S. with U.K. cycles, it does little to support the notion that U.S. cyclical changes have invariably preceded those in other economies in the recent past.

Of Sneezes and Colds. The tentative findings for the recent past do not support the popular notion that economic difficulties in the United States have been the source of subsequent difficulties in Europe. The popular theory that when the United States sneezes Europe catches cold needs to be reexamined.

The "sneeze hypothesis" means, presumably, that when the United States suffers a recession and a consequent reduction in its demand, including its demand for imports, this diminution in demand, relatively mild in U.S. terms, produces relatively severe contraction in the countries whose exports are thereby affected.[2] The sneeze hypothesis represents a particular version of what might be called the traditional hypothesis. The traditional hypothesis was well stated long ago by Wesley Clair Mitchell:

> Prosperity in any one country stimulates demand for the products of other countries, and so quickens the activities in the latter regions. . . . Further, prosperity . . . encourages investments abroad as well as at home, and the export of capital to other countries gives an impetus to their trade. A recession checks all these stimuli.[3]

Mitchell's notion would appear to make the chain of causation run from the country recovering earliest (or most strongly) to other economies. This generalization might, of course, be modified by differential degrees of dependence on imports or foreign capital investment. This notion, coupled with the recognition of the fact that

---

[2] The sneeze hypothesis is widely quoted, Charles Kindleberger attributes it to Sir Dennis Robertson among others. *Cf.* Charles P. Kindleberger, *International Economics*, 4th edition (Homewood, Ill.: Richard D. Irwin, Inc., 1968), p. 483.
[3] Mitchell, *Business Cycles: The Problem and Its Setting*, p. 446, quoted in Moore, "The State of the International Business Cycle," p. 22.

the United States was less dependent on exports than were other economies, may have led to the assumption that the sneeze was invariably America's and the cold, Europe's. With the United States and the United Kingdom used for illustrative purposes, the traditional hypothesis (as advanced by Mitchell) would lead one to expect (1) that U.S. exports to the United Kingdom would conform well to U.K. growth cycles, and (2) that U.K. exports to the United States would conform well to U.S. growth cycles. These expectations would be in accord with the presumed direct effects on imports of prosperity or recession in the importing country.

If, in addition, the United States exports its recessions, along the lines of the sneeze hypothesis, one might expect (3) that U.K. exports would conform well to U.K. growth cycles. On the other hand, if the contagion works in the opposite direction to that in which it is commonly held to work, one might expect (4) that U.S. exports would conform well to U.S. growth cycles. The sneeze hypothesis suggests that cyclical changes in the United States produce subsequent changes in other countries, and that these changes are more severe in the other countries than in the United States because they affect U.S. trade flows, which are more important to the other countries than to the United States.

All four of these expectations can be tested using the new growth-cycle chronologies and looking at trade between the United States and (in order) the United Kingdom, Japan, Canada, and West Germany. Table 8 shows the results of calculations testing the validity of both the traditional and the sneeze hypothesis for U.S.-U.K. trade. The traditional hypothesis is firmly supported. Column 2 shows that U.S. exports to the United Kingdom were very much influenced by U.K. cycles; U.K. import demand fluctuated with U.K. cycles, growing at a faster rate during U.K. upswings than during either preceding or succeeding downswings in all eight of the possible comparisons. The average annual growth of U.S. exports to the United Kingdom during U.K. upswings ($176 million) greatly exceeds the comparable average during U.K. downswings ($4 million). The reverse relationship is almost as sensitive; U.S. imports from the United Kingdom reflect fluctuations in U.S. demand based on U.S. cycles. Column 6 thus shows that during our upswings our imports from the United Kingdom increased by an average annual amount of $191 million. During our downswings our imports actually rose on average by $1 million. The traditional view that domestic cyclical developments provide the dominant influence on imports is clearly supported by the case of U.S.-U.K. trade during this period.

Table 8

AMOUNTS OF CHANGE IN U.S.-U.K. EXPORT TRADE DURING GROWTH CYCLES, 1951–1973

(in millions of current U.S. dollars)

U.K. Growth Cycle

U.K. Growth Cycle (1)		Annual Change In	
Upswings	Downswings	U.S. exports to United Kingdom (2)	U.K. exports to United States (3)
	1951–52	−220	+90
1952–55		+83	+35
	1955–58	−33	+85
1958–61		+100	+7
	1961–63	+10	+115
1963–66		+170	+243
	1966–67	+130	−60
1967–68		+350	+420
	1968–72	+132	+219
Average during			
Upswings		+176	+176
Downswings		+4	+90
Conformity index [a]		+100	0

U.S. Growth Cycle

U.S. Growth Cycle (4)		Annual Change In	
Upswings	Downswings	U.S. exports to United Kingdom (5)	U.K. exports to United States (6)
1952–53		+110	+35
	1953–54	+105	−25
1954–57		+138	+88
	1957–58	−280	+85
1958–60		+285	+75
	1960–61	−270	−130
1961–62		−10	+230
	1962–63	+30	0
1963–66		+170	+243
	1966–67	+130	−60
1967–69		+250	+185
	1969–70	+256	+134
1970–73		+343	+483
Average during			
Upswings		+184	+191
Downswings		−5	+1
Conformity index [a]		+67	+83

[a] A slower rate of growth during a growth cycle downswing than in an adjacent upswing is counted as an instance of positive conformity, the opposite as negative conformity. The number of positive instances less the number of negative instances, divided by the total number, times 100, is the conformity index. It can range from +100 to −100.

Source: Based on Table A-2.

Little or no support is found for the sneeze hypothesis, however. U.K. exports to the United States grew faster during U.K. upswings than they did during downswings only four out of eight times (column 3), and the average during upswings was larger than the average during downswings by a considerably smaller margin than was the case in column 2 (which reflects the traditional hypothesis). If this represents the impact on U.K. cycles of the ability or willingness of the United States to import U.K. goods, these U.S. "sneezes" hardly produced pneumonia.[4] Moreover, the "reverse sneeze"—that is, the impact on U.S. cycles of the cyclical changes in British imports from the United States—is, if anything, even stronger. Thus in column 5 the average annual change in U.S. exports to the United Kingdom during U.S. upswings is $184 million compared to an average decline of $5 million during U.S. downswings. But the significant finding is that neither column 3 nor column 5 gives much more support to either variant of the sneeze hypothesis than is given the traditional explanation of columns 2 and 6. (These conclusions are, of course, based on averages of absolute changes.)

Having commented at some length on the bearing of the U.S.-U.K. trade pattern on both of these hypotheses, we may briefly summarize the findings for Japan, Canada, and West Germany. We shall turn first to Canada (Table 9). It is well known that Canadian economic developments tend to reflect U.S. conditions somewhat more closely than do those of many other countries. Thus the validity of both the traditional and the sneeze hypothesis is of particular interest here, particularly in light of the indication in Table 6 that Canadian growth-cycle peaks customarily precede U.S. peaks while Canadian troughs lag U.S. troughs. The traditional hypothesis receives some support from the Canadian experience; column 2 shows that U.S. exports to Canada are far larger on the average during Canadian upswings ($555 million per year) than they are during Canadian downswings ($86 million per year). The conformity index is, however, somewhat lower in this case than in the case of swings in the Canadian economy.[5]

---

[4] Of course, some might argue that the British were merely anticipating U.S. expansions and contractions. While this may be true, further research, and of a more refined nature, would clearly be required to settle the matter. All that is being argued here is that the test under review does little if anything to support the sneeze hypothesis in any of its popular or simplistic forms.

[5] For a brief explanation of how conformity indexes are calculated, see footnote a to Table 8. In brief, a conformity index is a simple quantitative measure of the degree to which, and direction in which, changes in exports or imports reflect growth-cycle phases.

Table 9

AMOUNTS OF CHANGE IN U.S.-CANADIAN EXPORT TRADE DURING CYCLES, 1950–1973

(in millions of current U.S. dollars)

Canadian Growth Cycles (1) — Annual Change In

Upswings	Downswings	U.S. exports to Canada (2)	Canadian exports to United States (3)
1950–52		+380	+255
	1952–54	−5	+10
1954–56		+625	+245
	1956–58	−305	+40
1958–59		+310	+330
	1959–61	−35	−75
1961–62		+170	+330
	1962–63	+290	+130
1963–66		+817	+717
	1966–68	+720	+1370
1968–69		+1030	+1270
	1969–70	−150	+780
Average during Upswings		+555	+524
Average during Downswings		+86	+376
Conformity index		+82	+64

U.S. Growth Cycles (4) — Annual Change In

Upswings	Downswings	U.S. exports to Canada (5)	Canadian exports to United States (6)
1952–53		+230	+100
	1951–52	+190	+190
1954–57		+380	+210
	1953–54	−240	−800
1958–60		+150	+70
	1957–58	−500	−60
1961–62		+170	+330
	1960–61	−60	−40
1963–66		+817	+717
	1962–63	+290	+130
1967–69		+965	+1500
	1966–67	+540	+1010
1970–73		+1645a	+1570a
	1969–70	−150	+780
Average during Upswings		+622	+642
Average during Downswings		+10	+287
Conformity index		+85	+69

a Based on 1972 data.

Source: Based on Table A-3.

35

Table 10

RATES OF CHANGE IN U.S.-JAPANESE EXPORT TRADE DURING CYCLES, 1952–1973

(in millions of current U.S. dollars)

Japanese Growth Cycles (1)		Annual Change In		U.S. Growth Cycles (4)		Annual Change In	
Upswings	Downswings	U.S. exports to Japan (2)	Japanese exports to United States (3)	Upswings	Downswings	U.S. exports to Japan (5)	Japanese exports to United States (6)
	1954–55	−35	+170	1952–53		+50	0
1955–57		+292	+75		1953–54	+10	+50
	1957–59	−150	+222	1954–57		+183	+107
1959–61		+400	+10		1957–58	−390	+90
	1961–62	−320	+340	1958–60		+245	+208
1962–64		+295	+230		1960–61	+400	−40
1964–66		+586	+570	1961–62		−320	+340
	1966–70	+158	+716		1962–63	+280	+110
1970–72		+156	+1594	1963–66		+207	+497
					1966–67	+330	+40
				1967–69		+410	+985
					1969–70	+1192	+855
				1970–73		+1220	+1257
Average during Upswings		+393	+258			+285	+485
Average during Downswings		−87	+579			+304	+184
Conformity index		+100	−75			0	+83

Source: Based on Table A-4.

There is modest support for the sneeze hypothesis, in the sense that the average U.S. import from Canada appears to be higher during Canadian upswings than during Canadian downswings, though again the differential is far lower than in our examination of the traditional hypothesis. The conformity index is only 64. In any case, the U.S.-Canadian data support the sneeze hypothesis more strongly than do comparable data relating the United States to the other economies under review, but it is Canada that "sneezes"—not the United States. The reverse sneeze hypothesis is supported more impressively than the sneeze hypothesis. The average annual Canadian import from the United States shows a larger differential during U.S. upswings and U.S. downswings than is the case for any of the other three comparisons in Table 9. Moreover, the conformity index is the highest of all those shown in the table. This evidence, taken in conjunction with the evidence of Table 6, represents fairly strong presumptive support for the notion that customary explanations of U.S.-Canadian economic relations are somehow inadequate or misleading.

The two most rapidly growing market-oriented economies in the post-World-War-II period have been West Germany and Japan and for that reason the evidence concerning U.S. trade with them is especially interesting. The relevant information for Japan is shown in Table 10. Columns 2 and 6 give strong support to the traditional explanation of the relationship of trade to instability, with column 2 suggesting support for the impact of Japanese cycles on Japanese imports from the United States and column 6 showing considerable importance for U.S. imports from Japan emanating from U.S. cycles. The "sneeze hypothesis," considered in column 3, gets no support whatsoever in the case of Japan and indeed appears to be contradicted inasmuch as on the average U.S. imports from Japan actually increase during Japanese downswings. The reverse sneeze hypothesis is similarly contradicted by the Japanese evidence, if less decisively (column 5).

The German experience is shown in Table 11, and is consistent with the general tenor of the earlier findings. Columns 2 and 6 suggest that the German experience supports the traditional hypothesis concerning the dominant impact of domestic cycles on a country's import demand, while columns 3 and 5 give little support to either the sneeze or the reverse sneeze hypothesis.

The experience of U.S. trade with all four countries is summarized in Table 12. Here we have calculated the average annual change in U.S. exports to the foreign country and in foreign exports

Table 11

RATES OF CHANGE IN U.S.-W. GERMAN EXPORT TRADE DURING CYCLES, 1951–73
(in millions of current U.S. dollars)

W. German Growth Cycles (1) Upswings	Downswings	Annual Change In — U.S. exports to W. Germany (2)	German exports to United States (3)	U.S. Growth Cycles (4) Upswings	Downswings	Annual Change In — U.S. exports to W. Germany (5)	German exports to United States (6)
	1952–54	+28	+33		1951–52	—	—
1954–56		+219	+108	1952–53		−87	+65
	1956–59	−22	+142		1953–54	+142	+1
1959–61		+232	+32	1954–57		+275	+110
	1961–63	+120	+42		1957–58	−443	+22
1963–66		+31	+264	1958–60		+192	+139
	1966–67	+32	+159		1960–61	+71	−41
1967–70		+345	+392	1961–62		+238	+106
	1970–72	+34	+560		1962–63	+1	+41
1972–73		+948	+1094	1963–66		+31	+264
					1966–67	+32	+159
				1967–69		+218	+324
					1969–70	+598	+527
				1970–73		+339	+738
Average during Upswings		+355	+378			+172	+249
Downswings		+38	+179			+67	+118
Conformity index		+56	+11			+33	+83

Source: Based on Table A-5.

Table 12

SUMMARY: RATES OF CHANGE IN TRADE BETWEEN UNITED STATES AND FOUR DEVELOPED COUNTRIES DURING GROWTH CYCLES

(millions of current U.S. dollars, f.o.b.)

	Annual Amounts of Change in Exports	
	During foreign growth cycles	During U.S. growth cycles
U.S. exports to foreign countries		
Average during upswings	+386	+316
Average during downswings	+25	+91
Conformity index	+83	+47
Foreign exports to United States		
Average during upswings	+356	+392
Average during downswings	+252	+153
Conformity index	+6	+80

Notes: The four developed countries are the United Kingdom, Canada, Japan, and West Germany. Average of all annual averages available for all four countries. Conformity index comprises all positive conformity less all negative conformity, divided by total number of comparisons for the four countries, times 100.

Source: Tables 8 through 11.

to the United States during the foreign growth-cycle upswings and downswings and during the U.S. growth-cycle upswings and downswings. The summary conformity indexes have also been calculated. Testing the traditional hypothesis, we find that the average annual import during domestic growth-cycle upswings is significantly higher than the average annual import during domestic growth-cycle downswings and that the overall conformity indexes are quite high in both cases. The sneeze hypothesis receives no support from the average annual imports and the conformity index is insignificant. The reverse sneeze hypothesis receives more support than the sneeze hypothesis, but the support is not significant, as is made clear by the size of the conformity index.

Presumably the sneeze hypothesis is founded on the presumption that because of the obviously great size and importance of the U.S. economy, both absolutely and relative to other economies, what happens in the United States must necessarily affect what happens abroad. While this is surely true, it does not necessarily follow that cyclical developments in the United States necessarily cause subsequent cyclical changes in other countries in any direct or simplistic fashion or that changes in other countries cannot similarly affect changes in the United States. We have found little evidence to support the notion that U.S. cyclical developments have a dominant impact on cyclical changes in foreign countries through more or less coincident changes in U.S. imports. In fact, we have found as much or more support for the notion that foreign cyclical changes affect U.S. growth cycles by affecting U.S. exports. In all the cases examined, domestic cycles appear to affect import demand significantly, while the relation of domestic cycles to exports can accurately be characterized as tenuous at best. It should, of course, be underscored that the test discussed here is a crude one. Extension of this analysis to many more countries, with monthly or quarterly data, is clearly desirable.[6] Another refinement we hope to introduce will be to examine the behavior of trade flows for particular types of commodities or commodity groups among countries from the perspective of growth-cycle chronologies. We recognize, therefore, that far more detailed analysis is necessary before a viable positive explanation of the international economic interrelationships under consideration here can be offered. Such attention to detail may be necessary before any theory, including the sneeze hypothesis, can be definitively rejected. However, our evidence does very little to support the sneeze hypothesis. At the very least, an approach such as ours, even when based on an analysis of the behavior of total exports and imports, suggests that the underlying interrelationships and their impact on the international transmission of cyclical instability are far more complicated than is suggested by any facile explanation, including the sneeze hypothesis even in its most sophisticated forms, taking devaluations, breakdown by goods traded, and so on into account.

Even though the analysis made here has necessarily been crude, it should indicate the kind of work which the development of international growth-cycle chronologies can facilitate. While the development of leading indicators for growth cycles ought to enhance our understanding of how international instability is transmitted, this brief discussion suggests how we can find uses for the comparable growth-cycle chronologies and comparable indicators for a number of countries as envisioned by the International Economic Indicators project.

---

[6] It can be reported, however, that tentative initial studies conducted at the NBER with monthly data are entirely consistent with the findings reported in this section. They are described in the National Bureau's *Annual Report*, September 1975, in the report on the International Economic Indicators project by Geoffrey H. Moore and this author.

Is There an International Business Cycle? The evidence presented in Figures 1 and 2 suggests strongly that cycles in a number of market-oriented economies have often moved more or less in tandem. This agrees with older findings. Willard Thorp's 1926 *Business Annals* presented data on common cycle movements for some eighteen countries for the period 1790–1925. Wesley Clair Mitchell in his 1927 *Business Cycles: The Problem and Its Setting* suggested that there had been six international cycles between 1890 and 1926, or one every six years. Mitchell's explanation of these movements was quoted previously. Later, Oskar Morgenstern examined the United States, the United Kingdom, Germany, and France, and concluded that all four were in expansion together or in contraction together about half the time.[7] More recently, Ilse Mintz has worked on international cycles, particularly as they are manifested in trade flows. She developed a quarterly chronology of what she called a "world import cycle," for the period 1880–1959.[8] Finally, the Federal Reserve Bank of St. Louis has constructed a number of tables showing growth rates in several important measures of economic activity for ten important industrialized economies, based mostly on annual data.[9]

Recently Geoffrey H. Moore examined this information and reached a number of conclusions pertinent to our concerns here.[10] In twelve of the nineteen years from 1953 to 1973, the rate of change in the index of industrial production moved in the same direction for more than two-thirds of the nine countries he examined.[11] Moore then computed the median percentage change in the growth rates for each of the eight countries excluding the United States, as measured by the index of industrial production, by real GNP, by the value of imports, and by the value of exports. He then compared the consensus peaks and troughs in these measures for the eight countries with similar consensus peaks and troughs for the United States. The results are shown in Table 13.

---

[7] Oskar Morgenstern, *International Financial Transactions and Business Cycles* (Princeton, N.J.: Princeton University Press for National Bureau of Economic Research, 1959), pp. 40-46.

[8] Ilse Mintz, *Cyclical Fluctuations in the Exports of the United States Since 1879*, NBER, Studies in Business Cycles no. 15 (New York: Columbia University Press for the NBER, 1967), chapter 1.

[9] Federal Reserve Bank of St. Louis, "Rates of Change in Economic Data for Ten Industrial Countries," annual data, 1953-1972, October 1973.

[10] This summary of previous work on the international cycle including much of the subsequent discussion is from Geoffrey H. Moore, "The State of the International Business Cycle," *Business Economics*, September 1974, pp. 21-29.

[11] The countries were Belgium, Canada, France, Germany, Italy, Japan, Netherlands, the United Kingdom, and the United States.

Table 13

CONSENSUS PEAKS AND TROUGHS IN GROWTH RATES AS
MEASURED BY FOUR MEASURES OF ECONOMIC ACTIVITY,
EIGHT COUNTRIES OUTSIDE THE UNITED STATES AND
THE UNITED STATES, 1953–1973

Peaks		Troughs	
Eight countries	United States	Eight countries	United States
			1954
1955	1955	1958	1958
1960	1959	1961	1961
—	1962	—	1963
1964	1966	1967	1967
1969	1968	1971	1970
1973	1973		

Note: The eight countries are Belgium, Canada, France, West Germany, Italy, Japan, the Netherlands, and the United Kingdom. The four measures of economic growth are the index of industrial production, real GNP, the value of imports, and the value of exports.
Source: G. H. Moore, "The State of the International Business Cycle," *Business Economics,* September 1974, Table 2, p. 24.

Moore found a high correlation between the peaks and troughs in growth rates. The data set out in Table 13 show a consensus international cycle of four and a half years on the average, which is the same length Ilse Mintz found for her world import cycles during the period from 1879 to 1959. Moore's chronology does suggest that there may be a greater tendency for synchronous behavior between or among other countries than there is for synchronous behavior between those countries and the United States. However, it is difficult to be sure on the basis of this preliminary evidence. Clearly there is room for further exploration. Despite some differences, Moore finds considerable correlation between U.S. cycles and international cycles, with five of the turning point years the same, and three more within a year of each other. The period from 1962 to 1966 is conspicuous by virtue of the poor correspondence between cycles in the United States and cycles in other countries.

By concentrating on the peak and trough years indicated above, Moore is able to show that for his eight foreign countries and for the United States, the median rate of change for the variables he considers was always higher at peaks than at troughs. He shows that industrial and wholesale prices conformed well to the peaks (measurement being in rates of change), while only consumer prices conformed poorly. Finally, and bearing directly on the possibilities of developing reliable leading indicators of international cyclical activity, he shows that export orders for U.S. products (mostly durable goods and equipment), stock prices (for both the United States and the eight countries), and the money supply (for both the United States and the eight countries) conformed well to the international cycle dates selected. That is, these indicators led the cycles in the sense that the amplitude of their rates of change were large in the year before the reference peaks and small in the year before reference troughs.

The International Economic Indicator project at the National Bureau plans to examine the evidence for a "world cycle" in greater detail. We intend to compute some "industrial world cycle" composite indexes, beginning with a five-country composite index of leading, roughly coincident, and lagging indicators (the five countries being the United States, United Kingdom, Japan, Canada, and West Germany). Subsequently we plan to enlarge the composite indexes by adding other countries.

Clearly Moore's evidence is directly relevant to our work on international growth cycles, although it does not deal particularly with the problem of causation. It suggests the kind of research that must precede the effort to analyze the mechanisms by which international cyclical instability has been transmitted from country to country in the period after World War II. Moreover, like the findings previously considered, it suggests the value of studying modern international growth cycles.

CONCLUSIONS

The tendency to discount the distant past in considering the future is one against which researchers must generally be on guard. We have seen an important change in the character of cyclical instability from the period before World War II to the postwar period: recessions in many countries have been milder and shorter than before. Rapid growth rates, particularly when coupled with secular inflation, have combined to add a view of business cycles as recurring deviations from average growth rates to our traditional views of instability. In the postwar period a number of economies, notably that of West Germany, have exhibited very few classical cycles—that is, absolute declines in real economic activity. The United States has had the greatest number of classical cycles, but they have generally not been very severe. Research on West Germany, the United States, the United Kingdom, Canada, and Japan has suggested that developing a chronology of "growth cycles"—that is, deviation-from-trend cycles—should provide us with a valuable adjunct to the customary business-cycle chronologies of the past.

There is considerable evidence that growth cycles, whatever their cause, are best viewed as a modern manifestation of the same process that produced the business cycles of the past. Moreover, we have seen that the older "classical cycles" can still occur, as in the United States in the 1970s. We have suggested that much of the basis for the National Bureau's IEI project appears so far to have been valid. It has been possible, using the traditional techniques for selecting classical turning points, to select growth-cycle turning points, if the techniques are adjusted to measure cycles as deviations from longer-term trends. It does appear that the same kinds of economic activity that have proved reliable leading and lagging indicators of classical turning points may prove to be reliable leading and lagging indicators of growth-cycle turning points. The importance of these indicators should be substantial.

It should be possible to establish useful growth-cycle chronologies and to determine leading and confirming indicators of these chronologies for a number of industrialized market-oriented economies. There is consequently a real chance of making progress in studying the international transmission of cyclical instability. We have seen that there is a reasonable doubt whether the conventional view that instability spreads from the United States to the other countries is correct for the period since World War II.

Finally, there is growing evidence that, valuable as the addition of growth-cycle analysis may be, we shall have to continue to examine classical cycles, at least for the time being. The experience of the 1970s suggests that inflationary pressure was operating in tandem in most economies. The relatively severe classical recession in the United States appears to have been accompanied simultaneously by classical recessions in other industrialized market economies. This experience gives point to the search for reliable indicators for classical cycles and growth cycles—indicators which can be looked for in many economies, with a view to diagnosing and anticipating instability and toward understanding how it is transmitted from country to country. It is to be hoped that, as we learn to isolate and measure international cycles, we shall be able to make headway in ameliorating them as well.

APPENDIX

Table A-1

DETAILED INFORMATION ON TIMING COMPARISONS, UNITED STATES AND UNITED KINGDOM, AND UNITED STATES AND (WEST) GERMANY, SELECTED PERIODS, 1854–1969

	Number of Comparisons	Number of Extra Cycles	Number of Skipped Cycles	Number of Leads			Number of Lags			Number of Exact Coincidences
				Long	Short	Total	Long	Short	Total	
United States and United Kingdom										
Classical cycles										
1854–1938										
Peaks	14	1	5	1	3	4	5	5	10	0
Troughs	15	1	6	2	2	4	7	3	10	1
Peaks and troughs	29	2	11	3	5	8 (27.6%)	12	8	20 (69.0%)	1 (3.4%)
1854–1914										
Peaks	10	0	5	1	2	3	4	3	7	0
Troughs	11	0	5	1	1	2	6	2	8	1
Peaks and troughs	21	0	10	2	3	5 (23.8%)	10	5	15 (71.4%)	1 (4.8%)
1915–1938										
Peaks	5	1	1	0	1	1	2	2	4	0
Troughs	4	1	1	1	1	2	1	1	2	0
Peaks and troughs	9	2	2	1	2	3 (33.3%)	3	3	6 (60.7%)	0
Growth cycles										
1948–1969										
Peaks	5	0	2	3	1	4	1	0	1	0
Troughs	4	0	2	0	2	2	1	1	2	0
Peaks and troughs	9	0	4	3	3	6 (66.7%)	2	1	3 (33.3%)	0

Table A-1 (Continued)

	Number of Comparisons	Number of Extra Cycles	Number of Skipped Cycles	Number of Leads			Number of Lags			Number of Exact Coincidences
				Long	Short	Total	Long	Short	Total	
United States and (W.) Germany										
Classical cycles										
1879–1932										
Peaks	9	1	6	3	2	5	2	2	4	0
Troughs	10	1	6	3	1	4	5	1	6	0
Peaks and troughs	19	2	12	6	3	9	7	3	10	0
1879–1914										
Peaks	6	0	4	1	1	2	2	2	4	0
Troughs	7	0	4	1	1	2	5	0	5	0
Peaks and troughs	13	0	8	2	2	4	7	2	9	0
1915–1938										
Peaks	3	1	2	2	1	3	0	0	0	0
Troughs	3	1	2	2	0	2	0	1	1	0
Peaks and troughs	6	2	4	4	1	5	0	1	1	0
Growth cycles										
1950–1957										
Peaks	4	0	2	2	1	3	1	0	1	0
Troughs	4	0	2	2	1	3	1	0	1	0
Peaks and troughs	8	0	4	4	2	6	2	0	2	0

Source: Calculated from Tables 1 and 6.

47

Table A-2

U.K. EXPORTS TO THE UNITED STATES AND U.S. EXPORTS TO THE UNITED KINGDOM, 1951–1973

Year	U.K. Exports to United States (f.o.b. $ millions)	U.S. Exports to United Kingdom (f.o.b. $ millions)
1951	385	890
1952	410	670
1953	445	580
1954	420	685
1955	515	920
1956	680	900
1957	685	1,090
1958	770	820
1959	1,020	865
1960	920	1,390
1961	790	1,120
1962	1,020	1,110
1963	1,020	1,140
1964	1,140	1,580
1965	1,450	1,540
1966	1,750	1,650
1967	1,690	1,780
1968	2,110	2,130
1969	2,060	2,280
1970	2,194	2,536
1971	2,499	2,369
1972	2,987	2,658
1973	3,642	3,564

Note: For many years the U.N. has presented a table in the External Trade section of its *Statistical Yearbook,* entitled "World Export by Provenance and Destination." The exports from various countries and regions to other countries or regions are presented in millions of U.S. dollars valued f.o.b. at the border of the exporting country, in accordance with recommendations of the U.N. Economic and Social Council. They are therefore valued by transaction value (a current dollar concept) adjusted for certain transportation and insurance charges paid by the importing country to the exporting country.

Data for 1951-1960 are from Table 150, p. 418, in the 1961 *Yearbook.* Later years are from the 1973 *Yearbook,* Table 144. Data are revised and an attempt has been made here to present the latest data for each year.

Source: *U.N. Statistical Yearbook,* various years. (See note above.)

Table A-3

CANADIAN EXPORTS TO THE UNITED STATES AND U.S. EXPORTS TO CANADA, 1950–1972
(current U.S. dollars)

Year	Canadian Exports to United States (f.o.b. $ millions)	U.S. Exports to Canada (f.o.b. $ millions)
1950	1,900	1,950
1951	2,220	2,520
1952	2,410	2,710
1953	2,510	2,940
1954	2,430	2,700
1955	2,640	3,140
1956	2,920	3,950
1957	3,060	3,840
1958	3,000	3,340
1959	3,330	3,650
1960	3,140	3,640
1961	3,180	3,580
1962	3,510	3,750
1963	3,640	4,040
1964	4,120	4,830
1965	4,670	5,490
1966	5,790	6,490
1967	6,800	7,030
1968	8,530	7,930
1969	9,800	8,960
1970	10,580	8,810
1971	12,080	10,100
1972	13,720	12,100

Source: *U.N. Statistical Yearbook.* See note to Table A-2.

Table A-4

JAPANESE EXPORTS TO THE UNITED STATES AND U.S. EXPORTS TO JAPAN, 1950–1973
(current U.S. dollars)

Year	U.S. Exports to Japan (f.o.b. $ millions)	Japanese Exports to United States (f.o.b. $ millions)
1950	415	185
1951	595	190
1952	620	235
1953	670	235
1954	680	285
1955	645	455
1956	900	550
1957	1,230	605
1958	840	695
1959	930	1,050
1960	1,330	1,110
1961	1,730	1,070
1962	1,410	1,410
1963	1,690	1,520
1964	2,000	1,870
1965	2,040	2,510
1966	2,310	3,010
1967	2,640	3,050
1968	2,920	4,130
1969	3,460	5,020
1970	4,652	5,875
1971	4,055	7,259
1972	4,963	9,064
1973	8,312	9,645

Source: *U.N. Statistical Yearbook.* See note to Table A-2.

Table A-5

W. GERMAN EXPORTS TO THE UNITED STATES AND
U.S. EXPORTS TO W. GERMANY, 1952–1974
(current U.S. dollars)

Year	U.S. Exports to W. Germany (f.o.b. $ millions)	W. German Exports to United States (f.o.b. $ millions)
1952	450	212
1953	363	277
1954	505	278
1955	607	366
1956	943	494
1957	1,330	607
1958	887	629
1959	878	920
1960	1,272	897
1961	1,343	856
1962	1,581	962
1963	1,582	1,003
1964	1,606	1,191
1965	1,650	1,341
1966	1,674	1,796
1967	1,706	1,955
1968	1,709	2,721
1969	2,142	2,603
1970	2,740	3,130
1971	2,831	3,650
1972	2,808	4,250
1973	3,756	5,344
1974	4,986	6,428

Source: For 1952-1966, Department of Commerce, Bureau of Census, *Highlights of U.S. Export and Import Trade,* Aug. 1967. Thereafter *ibid.,* annually, December issue.